W9-AVI-861

FOLLOW THE LEADER STORIES

Forgive, Joseph!

CAROLYN NYSTROM

Illustrated by Sharon Dahl

MOODY PRESS
CHICAGO

j222.11
NYS

Carolyn Nystrom is well known as the author of Moody Press's long-lived doctrinal series, Children's Bible Basics. She has written 64 books—some available in ten languages—as well as stories and curriculum material. A former elementary school teacher, she also served on the curriculum committee of her local school board.

Carolyn and her husband, Roger, live in St. Charles, Illinois, a Chicago suburb. As foster parents, they have cared for seven children in addition to their own two daughters. In her spare time, Carolyn enjoys hiking, classical music, gardening, aerobics, and making quilts.

Now award-winning artist Sharon Dahl has teamed up with Carolyn Nystrom to provide lively, captivating illustrations for the Follow the Leader Series. Sharon lives with her husband Gordon and daughters Samantha and Sydney in Boonton Township, New Jersey.

©1998 by
CAROLYN NYSTROM

PD OP

All rights reserved. No part of this book may be reproduced in any form without permission in writing from the publisher, except in the case of brief quotations embodied in critical articles or reviews.

Moody Press, a ministry of the Moody Bible Institute, is designed for education, evangelization, and edification. If we may assist you in knowing more about Christ and the Christian life, please write us without obligation: Moody Press, c/o MLM, Chicago, IL 60610.

ISBN: 0-8024-2207-1

1 3 5 7 9 10 8 6 4 2

Printed in the United States of America

I really liked my coat. My father gave it to me. It had a hundred colors that shimmered in the light when I ran. When I wrapped my coat around me at night, I felt as if my father held me in his arms and whispered, "I love you." But that coat got me in a lot of trouble.

One night I dreamed that I was working in the field with my eleven brothers. We were tying bundles of grain. Then my bundle stood tall while their bundles bowed low. Another time I dreamed that eleven stars and even the moon and sun bowed down to me.

My brothers didn't like those dreams. They growled, "So you think you will be our king, do you?" My father said, "Will your mother and I bow to you, too?"

My brothers hated me because of my coat and my dreams and my father's love.

"I need your help," my father said one day. "Go check on your brothers. Let me know if they are taking good care of the sheep."

I was a little scared. There were lots of brothers and only one of me. What if I gave my father a bad report about them—as I had another time? Would they hate me even more?

Finally I saw my brothers far away with lots and lots of sheep. They saw me too, but they did not wave. I could see them knotted together talking, talking. I walked closer.

Suddenly I felt my feet thrown high in the air. My coat was yanked off. Then down, down, down I went until everything was dark—except for a hole of light at the top.

I could hear them talking far above.

"We'll just leave him there."

"No, he'll die."

"So what?"

"He's our brother!"

"Yeh, brother Joseph!" one of them spat.

"What about Father?"

"We'll say he's dead."

"He won't believe us."

"He knows we hate him."

"We'll prove he's dead."

"How?"

"With the coat."

"We'll tear it up and say a wild animal got him."

"And we're so sad." They laughed.

But I didn't die. Brother Judah came to my rescue.
"Let's sell him instead," he said. "At least we'll get money."

Soon I was on my way to Egypt—as a slave. I travelled with a large caravan of men and camels. But slaves don't ride camels. Slaves walk—behind the camels. I wondered if I would ever see home again. I worried about my father. I knew he would be sad.

In Egypt the men spread out all the things they wanted to sell: rugs, bells, spices, and me. A man named Potiphar bought me to help him with his work. But God was with me, even in Egypt. Potiphar liked my hard work. Soon he put me in charge of almost everything he had. He trusted me.

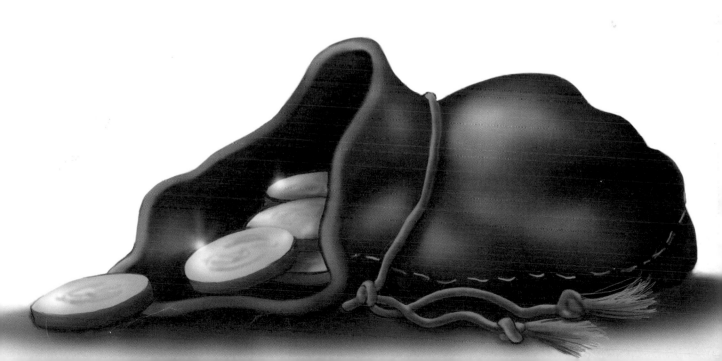

Potiphar's wife liked me, too. She would say, "Oh, you are so handsome. Oh, please come and sit next to me."

I would say, "I have something important to do right now for your husband."

But one day she grabbed my cloak. "Come to bed with me," she said.

"How could I do such a terrible thing!" I answered. "That is a sin against God, and it is not fair to your husband." She kept holding onto my cloak, but I ran out of the house as fast as I could.

Soon I heard screams from the house. "Joseph tried to hurt me," she cried, "and here is his cloak."

That's how I wound up in jail.

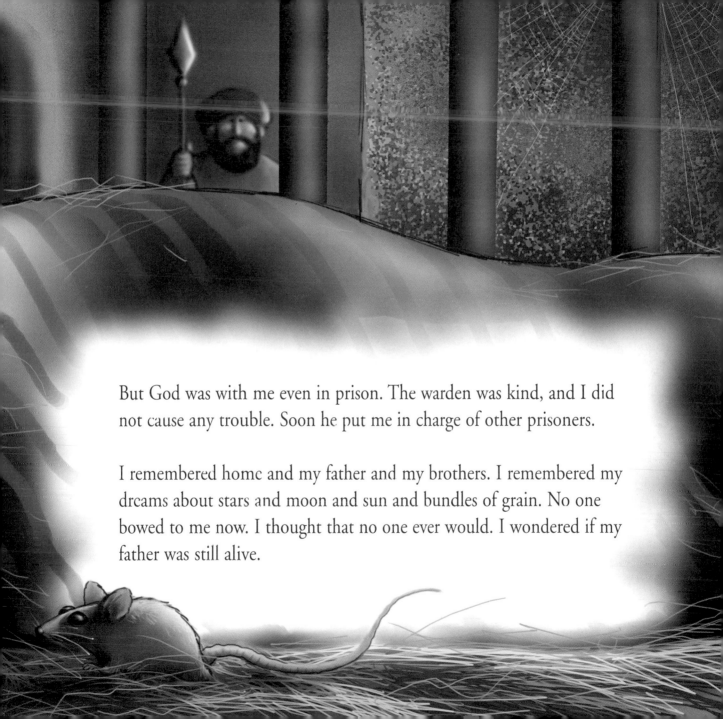

But God was with me even in prison. The warden was kind, and I did not cause any trouble. Soon he put me in charge of other prisoners.

I remembered home and my father and my brothers. I remembered my dreams about stars and moon and sun and bundles of grain. No one bowed to me now. I thought that no one ever would. I wondered if my father was still alive.

And then the king of Egypt got angry at his butler and his baker. So he sent them to jail. One morning they looked extra sad. "What's wrong?" I asked.

"Last night we dreamed strange dreams," they said.

"In my dream," said the butler, "I saw three branches of grapes, and I was serving the king again."

"Your dream is true," I answered. "God has shown me what it means. In three days the king will bring you back to work for him."

The baker said, "In my dream, I carried three baskets of bread on my head—and wild birds pecked at the bread."

"Your dream is also true. In three days the king will kill you. I'm sorry."

In three days it all happened just the way I said. The baker died. The butler went back to work. He forgot about prison and me.

After two years, the king had two dreams that worried him. None of his wise men could tell him what the dreams meant. Finally the butler remembered me. I shaved, washed, and dressed, and they took me to see the king.

"I hear that you can tell what dreams mean," the king said.

"I can't do it," I explained. "But God will show me what He wants you to know."

"I dreamed that seven fat cows came out of the river," the king said. "But seven thin cows came and ate them up. Then I saw seven full heads of grain on a single stalk. But seven thin heads of grain swallowed them up."

"God is showing you what He is about to do," I said. "Egypt will have seven good years. But after that will come seven years when nothing will grow. Animals will die. People will be hungry."

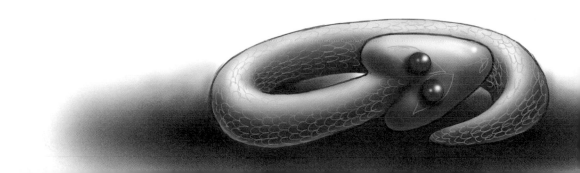

"Help us get ready," the king said. "God has shown you the meaning of my dreams. Maybe He will also show you how to prepare our nation for famine."

That was my last day in jail. The king put me in charge of all the food in the whole land. I taught people how to save so that each city had a mountain of food piled high. The king gave me fine clothes, a gold chain, a chariot, and even a wife. God gave us two sons, whom I loved. Then the seven good years came to an end.

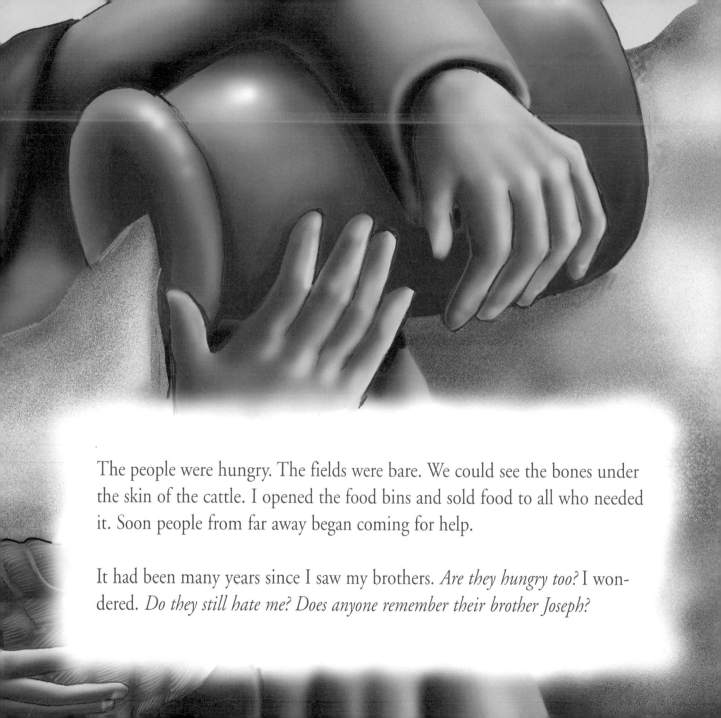

The people were hungry. The fields were bare. We could see the bones under the skin of the cattle. I opened the food bins and sold food to all who needed it. Soon people from far away began coming for help.

It had been many years since I saw my brothers. *Are they hungry too?* I wondered. *Do they still hate me? Does anyone remember their brother Joseph?*

Then one day I saw them walking slowly toward me. They looked old and thin and very tired. They bowed low and said, "Please, sir, we are hungry. May we buy food for our family?"

"Who is your family?" I asked.

"We are twelve brothers," they answered. "Benjamin, the youngest, is at home with our father."

"And the other?" I asked.

"The other is . . . is . . . gone," one said.

I remembered the mocking, the pit, and how they sold me. "You are spies!" I shouted. "Guards, take these men to jail."

But I also remembered my dreams from God. Three days later I brought my brothers out and said, "Go home with your food. But if you come back, you must bring your brother Benjamin. And I will keep Simeon here in jail."

I heard them whisper to each other, "God is punishing us because of what we did to brother Joseph."

I turned away and cried.

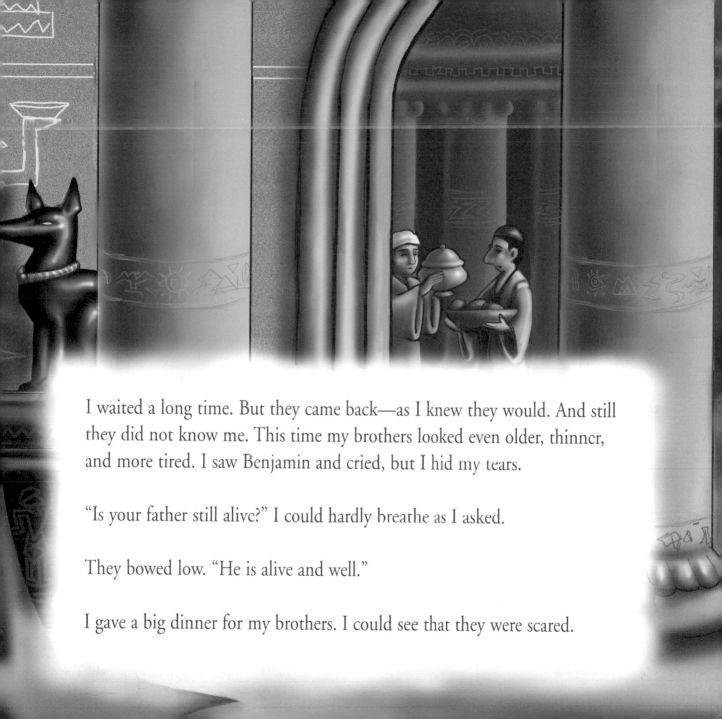

I waited a long time. But they came back—as I knew they would. And still they did not know me. This time my brothers looked even older, thinner, and more tired. I saw Benjamin and cried, but I hid my tears.

"Is your father still alive?" I could hardly breathe as I asked.

They bowed low. "He is alive and well."

I gave a big dinner for my brothers. I could see that they were scared.

Next morning I told my servant to fill their sacks with grain, to put all their money into the sacks—and to hide my silver cup in Benjamin's sack. I said good-bye to my brothers, but I knew they would be back.

Later I told my servant, "Go after them. Tell them that someone has stolen my cup. Search their bags. Tell them that the man who has my cup will be my slave!" Had my brothers changed? I would soon know.

They stumbled into the room. "Please, sir. Let all the rest of us be your slaves," they said. "Not this young one. Our father would die of sadness."

"No, no," Judah begged. "Let all my brothers go home. I will be your slave."

"Leave," I told my servants. "Leave now!"
Then I said, "I am your brother Joseph! Is our father really still alive?"

My brothers pulled away from me. I could see fear on every face.
"But . . . but . . . we thought . . ." someone began.
"Yes, I know," I said. "You sold me as a slave."
"But you are not . . ."

"No, I am not a slave. Not now." I sighed, remembering Potiphar and prison.
"But God sent me here ahead of you so that I could help you. You couldn't know
that. And neither could I."
Finally the fear began to leave their faces.

"There are five more years of famine to come," I told them. "Bring our father and live here with me. I will give you the best land."

That's how my people came to live in Egypt—seventy of us in all! We were a family again. And I was brother Joseph.

I knew that, a long time ago, my brothers tried to hurt me—and they did. But God meant it for good. And good is what happened.